"There's a lot packed into this colorful title that falls somewhere between self-help and peer advice."
— *School Library Journal*

Real Friends vs. the Other Kind

MIDDLE SCHOOL CONFIDENTIAL™

BOOK 2

ANNIE FOX, M.Ed.

free spirit
PUBLISHING®

Library of Congress Cataloging-in-Publication Data
Fox, Annie, 1950–
  Real friends vs. the other kind / Annie Fox.
    p. cm. — (Middle school confidential)
  Includes index.
  ISBN-13: 978-1-57542-319-7
1. Friendship in children—Juvenile literature. 2. Interpersonal relations in children—Juv
literature. 3. Middle school students—Psychology. I. Title. II. Title: Real friends versus the other
  BF723.F68F69 2009
  177'.62083—dc22

                                                                    200803136

Reading Level Grades 7 & Up; Interest Level Ages 11–14; Fountas & Pinnell Guided Reading Le

Edited by Douglas J. Fehlen
Cover design and illustration by Matt Kindt
Interior design by Tasha Kenyon

10 9 8 7 6 5 4 3 2
Printed in Hong Kong
P17200110

Free Spirit Publishing Inc.
217 Fifth Avenue North, Suite 200
Minneapolis, MN 55401-1299
(612) 338-2068
help4kids@freespirit.com
www.freespirit.com

edication

erra's online friends around the world, this book is for you. Thanks for trusting me with
problems, wishes, and dreams. Thanks also for responding so honestly to my question-
es. May all of your friendships always be real ones.

knowledgments

ks don't write themselves no matter how clever their characters are. Authors don't
k alone either. I have many people to thank for their creativity and hard work in the
elopment of this book series. I like to think of them as "Friends of Middle School
fidential." They include: Matt Kindt (brilliant illustrator), Douglas Fehlen (tireless
or), Tasha Kenyon (dynamic graphic designer), Judy Galbraith (compassionate
isher), and the rest of the fantastic Free Spirit team. I am so fortunate to have found
me with you good people!

Thanks also to Marin County librarians Shereen Ash, Bonnie Gosliner, and Amanda
st. I appreciate your research on my behalf. Your teen fiction recommendations pro-
d me with some great reads.

Finally, I want to thank my husband, David Fox, who is the best friend I'll ever have.

Contents

ntroduction

Hi. I'm an online advisor at a Web site for teens (www.theinsite.org). I get a lot of email from visitors of the site about things going on in their lives. Friendships come up more than any other topic. "He acts like he doesn't want to be my friend anymore." "She's spreading rumors." "He always ditches me."

It usually boils down to, "My friend isn't being a friend. What do I do?"

One thing's for sure: You can't change the way someone is acting. No one has that power over anybody else. But the key to your friendships is *you* and the choices you make. If you don't like what's going on, you can change the way you handle a situation, or the way you deal with your feelings. If it becomes necessary, you can even change friends.

The fact is we all want, need, and deserve friends who accept and respect us for who we are. But where do you find them? How do you hang on to them? And what do you do if it feels like someone could be more than a friend?

The short answer: Keep reading. You can find out a lot about relationships right here in the stories of six teens with their own friendship dilemmas. You'll also find quotes and advice from real teens, quizzes, tips, and insider tools for making friendships stronger. If you have any questions that aren't addressed in this book, feel free to email me at help4kids@freespirit.com. I'd also enjoy hearing any stories or suggestions of your own.

In friendship,
Annie

There's nothing like being with friends.
But if you're like us, you've probably wondered about some friendships. Maybe you're not sure if someone is a real friend or the "other" kind. Speaking of which, a few weeks ago a kid from Chris's old school showed up at the park....

helle, who's really smart, just couldn't pass
. one up. So she asked one of her famous
ɔing questions:

> **WHAT EXACTLY DO WE MEAN WHEN WE CALL SOMEONE A FRIEND?**

meone you trust. Someone who
s you. Someone who's fun to be
ɹ. We all had different answers.
. after a while it seemed like we
en't completely sure. Maybe it's
ause sometimes friendships can be
ly confusing. Especially when the
ple you think are friends start acting
 something else.
Why do friends have problems with one
ther? We didn't have a clue. But like Michelle
s, "Just because you don't know the answers doesn't
an there aren't any!" That made sense, so we decided to ask
er teens how they handle friendship issues. Some even had advice for when
ple want to be more than friends—something we're even more clueless about.
Turns out we received a lot of insider information for surviving the social scene
middle school. That's why this series is called "Middle School Confidential"—
ause not everyone knows what we've found out. Like how to keep relationships
ly strong.

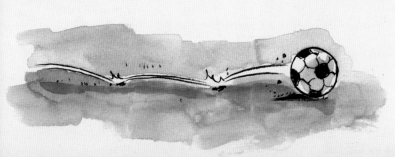

Not that tough situations no longer come up between friends—they do. But, as we've learned, there are a lot of helpful things you can do to get through the rough spots.

Jack

Abby

Mateo

CUTE!

OOH . . . CUTE!

JACK, YOU OKAY?

YEAH, CHRIS. JUST THINKING ABOUT MY DOG, SAMMI.

SHE DIED BEFORE WE MOVED HERE. I MISS HER.

MISS WHO?

HIS DOG.

MY *FRIEND*.

A FRIEND IS A PERSON WHO CARES ABOUT YOU. TECHNICALLY A DOG IS A PET.

WRONG, MICHELLE. SAMMI WAS MY FRIEND.

WHO'S SAMMI?

DUNNO. I MISSED THAT PART.

CAN SOMEONE HIT REWIND?

When things are cool between you and friends, you probably aren't thinking much about why you like each other. You just do. And since most friendships just seem to start up on their own, you may have never thought about what it is you look for in a friend.

But suppose you're in a situation where you or a friend has recently moved, or moved apart. If you are looking for new people to hang out with—or you're taking a new look at the friends you have—you might wonder what makes a good friend. Is it important that a person is honest? Funny? Into sports? Should you agree all the time?

There are many ways to define friendship, but if you're looking for real friends (instead of the other kind) you might want to think about what it means to you. Because just like shopping for anything new, the more you know about what you're looking for, the easier it can be to find.

From the "real friend" FILES

"For me a friend is a helpful person I can laugh with."
—Jake, 13

"You need to know your real friends will cheer you up when you're down."
—Jasmine, 12

"The friends I'm closest with are always truthful, even when the truth may hurt. They are always looking out for my best interests."
—Lucia, 14

"A friend is someone I don't need to feel competitive with."
—Richard, 13

"I appreciate friends I can talk to without any frustration."
—Karl, 12

"Real friends are there when I need them most. They know when something is wrong, even if I'm smiling and saying everything is fine."
—Felice, 13

"A true friend has my back and will stick with me no matter what. He keeps my business private, and he appreciates and respects me."
—Justin, 11

Real Friend? or the Other Kind?

It can be hard to know exactly w qualities to look for in other people here are some ideas to consider wh comes to friends:

1. **Real friends are honest.** You not always like or agree with they say, but you can always that they're telling you the truth.

2. **Real friends care.** They try to you in any way they can. What they do in the friendship they because you matter to them.

3. **Real friends accept you.** W you're with them, there's no pres to pretend to be someone you're

4. **Real friends respect you.** They ten to what you have to say and always consider your ideas, o ions, and feelings.

5. **Real friends get you.** They un stand who you are. They also k what's important to you so you d have to do a lot of extra explaini

6. **Real friends forgive one ano** No one is perfect. Real friends k this and forgive one another w mistakes are made.

When you have trust in a friendship, you don't even have to think about it. But the minute someone does something you don't expect, you probably notice right away. For example, suppose you tell your best friend something embarrassing and he swears he won't tell anyone. But then he does! Or if you screw up during a game and a girl you thought was a friend starts piling insults on you. Situations like that might make you wonder what's going on. That's why the way people treat you and how you feel when you're with them says a lot about the kind of friends they are.

"That's why we're friends"

"Some people you kind of have to be careful with when it comes to what you say. But with my best friend I can always be myself."
—Marianna, 12

"I have a buddy who knows just what to say at the right time. He always has the right attitude—no matter where he is or what's happening. He's like my role model."
—Javier, 14

"One of my good friends has a very bubbly personality and makes everyone feel welcome. She's got this aura that follows her everywhere, and being with her makes me feel more confident."
—Bethany, 13

"I know this guy who makes people fe there's a reason for them to be who th are—like he genuinely cares about the He makes me feel proud of myself, an gives me hope when I feel down."
—Lorena, 13

"My best friend is a crazy, cool, all-around good guy. We do everything together and he always makes me laugh."
—Jonah, 12

"My best friend and I are so alike. She the only person who actually understar me. Sometimes it feels like she can re my mind."
—Wynette, 11

Evaluate your friendship network to see how your friends measure up. It's best to do this on your own. You might not be honest if people are looking over your shoulder.

1. Get a piece of notebook paper. **Draw four long columns on the page.**

2. Write these words at the top of the columns: **My Friends, Always, Sometimes, Never.**

3. In the first column list of all your friends. For each one, ask yourself: **Is this person always, sometimes, or never my real friend?**

   —**Always friends respect and support you pretty much all the time. If they do slip up, they are quick to apologize and they try to avoid making the same mistake. They're also helpful, loyal, and trustworthy.**

   —**Sometimes friends are friends only when it's convenient for them.**

   —**Never friends are not real friends. Maybe they once were, but now. . . not really.**

4. Place a checkmark in the column that best matches the kind of friend a person is.
   Always? Sometimes? Never?

5. Whatcha got? **If you have Never friends, you deserve better. If you have Sometimes friends, you may need to speak up more often when they don't treat you right. If you have at least one Always friend, then you've got gold. Want more Always friends? You may have to raise the bar when it comes to what you ask of others—and of yourself.**

   Think about it: If your friends did this exercise, where would they put you?

Because you and each of your friends are unique, there's no single "right" way to have a great friendship. You're going to do it your way, and that's the way it should be. As long as you and your friends have two-way trust, then everything else is probably going to work just fine.

Speaking of two-way trust, don't forget about trusting yourself because that's a big part of any friendship. You might want to ask, "When it comes to friends, do I always trust my own feelings?" Feelings are like your personal sensor for what's going on in a friendship. They can pretty much tell you instantly when someone's treating you with respect and when they're not. **And while you're paying attention to the way people treat you, check out the kind of friendship you're giving back.**

BECAUSE THAT'S WHAT REAL FRIENDS DO!

noticed that a friend of mine was feeling and lonely. I felt bad for him, so I started hang out with him more often."
odd, 13

me of my friends started feeling like I'd ditching them to spend all of my time other people. I didn't want that, so we red out a system where I could hang out everyone."
inah, 12

friend was sneaking out to chill with her r brother's friend. I was really worried. en I knew she was out, I called her house her mom discovered she wasn't there. irst my friend hated me for it. Now she nks me for what I did."
arter, 14

"My friend was into some bad things, so I told her older sister. My friend was mad and said, 'Friends don't betray friends!' I told her that I was sorry I broke her trust. She's still mad, but I think I did the right thing."
—Bing, 13

"My friend's parents were going through a divorce, and she was upset all the time. I gave her a shoulder to cry on and lots of advice."
—Pam, 12

"When I found out one of my friends had gotten a high score on something, I was really proud of her and not at all jealous. I think that's what a really good friend should be."
—Devora, 11

The Complete Idiot's Guide to Friendship for Teens by Ericka Lutz. Learn the ins and outs of making and keeping friends and overcoming friendship challenges. Tips and suggestions offer practical advice for choosing new friends while staying loyal to those you have.

Holes by Louis Sachar. In a case of mistaken identity, Stanley Yelnats ends up in a juvenile detention facility. Camp Green Lake is a place where guys are sent to dig holes to keep them out of trouble. But what are the holes for? Find out in this book of intrigue and friendship.

The Sisterhood of the Traveling Pants by Ann Brashares. One pair of "magical" jeans perfectly fits four close friends of very different sizes. But there's more: The jeans connect the girls across great distances during a summer of major challenges.

Having real friends in your network can make life easier and a lot more fun.

When you know how a real friend is supposed to act, then you can see friendships for what they really are. If you or your friends aren't always the real kind, then you probably want to talk about what's going on. **Why? Because you deserve to have people in your life who support you 100 percent—and your friends deserve the same from you.**

It would be truly amazing if you and your friends never hurt or disappointed each other.
But disappointments happen from time to time—even with best friends. Sometimes people may upset you (by accident or on purpose). And sometimes you may do the same to them. That's not how friends should treat each other, so what's going on?

Maybe someone is in a bad mood and you just happen to be there. Or maybe a friend has an annoying habit that you've never mentioned, but one day you've had enough and you lose control. At those moments respect and trust might go missing in action, and what's left may not be a pretty sight.

WASN'T SUCH A GOOD FRIEND

THERE ARE AS MANY WAYS TO BE A BAD FRIEND AS THERE ARE TO BE A GOOD ONE!

"I teased my friend really bad about a girl liking him."
—Raymond, 11

"Some of my friends started smoking. I was going to ask them to stop, but I didn't wanna get in their business."
—Rory, 13

"I was really mad at my best friend 'cause I thought she was ditching me, so I told one of her secrets to someone I knew she hated."
—Marianne, 12

"I told an embarrassing story about my friend. He ended up hearing part of it and got really mad."
—Arno, 13

"I lied to my friend about having a busy weekend, but really, I just didn't want to hang out with her. Not great, huh?"
—Petra, 12

"I went out with the girl my friend liked. I feel bad about that."
—Hugo, 14

"I started rumors to get back at a friend. I was happy until I realized how much it hurt her. I was being stupid!"
—Linda, 12

DON'T ADD
to the Garbage

There's garbage that goes in the trash, and there's social garbage —
teasing, lying, ditching, rumors . . . you get the idea. If someone
betrays you, it's normal to feel angry or hurt. But if you try to get
back at the person, you are only adding to the garbage pile. Try this
when you're tempted to get revenge:

1. **Stop.** Before you do something that will make a situation worse,
   take a break.

2. **Breathe.** Close your eyes. Breathe in slowly through your nose and
   think, "Breathing in." Breathe out slowly through your mouth and
   think, "Breathing out." Repeat 4–5 times.

3. **Think.** "Will this show that I'm a good friend or create more problems?" If you don't want more garbage, then don't add to it. Should
   you let friends disrespect you? No way! But going negative isn't the
   answer either. Revenge is never cool, so what should you do?

4. **Talk to your friend privately and calmly.** Explain how you feel
   about what happened. Need to apologize for anything you did (or
   failed to do)? Now's the time.

5. **Listen to the other side.** Show that you sincerely want to hear
   what your friend has to say and there's a good chance the person
   will show you respect.

6. **Strengthen a friendship.** Discussing what happened can lead to
   fewer problems in the future. If you two can't repair the damage, at
   least you'll know that you did the right thing by trying.

How are you supposed to feel when some-one you trust lets you down?

For example, imagine that you and a friend usually have a good time playing video games. But then one day when you're winning, he accuses you of cheating and throws your controller against the wall. Or if you tell someone that you didn't appreciate a rude comment and she gets mad and says you're trying to ruin the friendship. In either case, that's probably going to feel very weird. And you may not know what to do because suddenly you can't count on how the other person will react.

One thing you *can* count on is that problems come up between people. They come up between friends and between people who don't know each other. When someone insults you or hurts your feelings it isn't always easy to stay calm. You could go on the attack. Or you could choose to do something that's more likely to help the situation.

Do something different

"I was with my friend and we were about to get into something. I backed away and told him to chill out. I mean what's the point of getting into a fight?"
—Ray, 13

"My ex-best friend sent me a mean email. Instead of engaging, I didn't respond or let her know I was upset."
—Sari, 12

"Our team won a volleyball tournament. When we came to shake hands at the end of the game, the girls I knew on the other team wouldn't shake my hand. Usually I would have talked trash about them, but I realized it was just going to make things worse. I let it go instead."
—Denise, 11

"I've had apple chunks spit on me b 'friend.' I was upset, but I didn't do anyth I wouldn't stoop to that level."
—Noah, 14

"My friend was acting like a jerk, so I v out and took a run."
—Tony, 13

"I made a joke that my friend didn't funny. During P.E. she gave me the si treatment. Later, I called her and found why she was so angry. I apologized and her I'd never do it again. Now she's spr ing mean rumors about me behind my b I'm just trying to avoid her until she bu up and apologizes."
—Mina, 12

hat Would a
eal Friend Do?

u and a friend are arguing about something when you accidentally let a mean mment slip out. You:

- say you were just kidding.
- sincerely apologize and promise to try not to let it happen again.
- act like it never happened.
- keep saying it whenever you're mad at your friend.

friend played great in a game you didn't do so well in. You:

- say, "Yeah, well, the other team wasn't very good."
- brag about how well you played last week.
- act like you're mad.
- congratulate your friend on a game well played.

omeone says a friend made mean comments about you. You:

- say nothing and pretend you never heard it.
- try to get even.
- stop talking to the person, but don't say why you're mad.
- talk to your friend and find out the truth.

friend wants to talk about a problem, but you just got a text message. You:

- give your friend 100 percent of your attention.
- ask, "Can we talk about this later?" and then start texting.
- have a text conversation as the person talks.
- listen to your friend—then send out a mass message with the latest gossip.

our friend just decided to audition for the same acting role that you've been lking about for six weeks. You:

- pretend that you don't mind when you really do.
- act mad without telling your friend why.
- tell your friend how you really feel.
- decide not to try out for the play.

Answers:

1. **b.** Real friends may lose control from time to time, but they are quick to apologize. And they make a real effort not to make the same mistake again.

2. **d.** Real friends support each other's successes. They are genuinely happy when a buddy has a win.

3. **d.** Real friends are interested in understanding why conflicts happen so that they can get to the bottom of them and make friendships stronger.

4. **a.** Real friends show respect and support by focusing and really listening to each other. They also don't spread information shared in confidence.

5. **c.** Real friends care about each other. They can't show they care unless they tell each other how they really feel about what's going on.

When conflicts come up between you and friends, it's easy to get defensive and blame it all on them. But that kind of thinking rarely helps. And it's pretty much never true that they're 100 percent wrong and you're 100 percent right. Even if you didn't personally start the argument this time, you've probably contributed to a fight before. Besides, "who started it" is not as important as how you work together to make peace and get the friendship rolling again.

To do your part (which is the only part you get), you may have to admit that sometimes you make mistakes. After all, everybody does. That's why apologies were invented.

APOLOGIES . . .

If saying you're sorry isn't always easy for you, you're not alone. At certain times the words can get stuck in everyone's throat. Even so, when you realize that you've done something (accidentally or on purpose) that hurt a friend or damaged a friendship, you need to apologize. These tips can help:

1. **Take responsibility.** Hurting people isn't cool, no matter what they might have done. When you realize that you added to a conflict, own up to it.

2. **Chill.** If the thought of apologizing stresses you out, take a break. Shoot some hoops. Take a walk or go for a run. Play a game. Journal. Do whatever it takes to calm down and clear your mind.

3. **Think, "Why did I do that?"** Not sure? Then play detective and get some answers. What did the person do that made you so angry, hurt, or jealous that you went on the attack?

4. **Talk to your friend face to face, in priv** That shows respect. Besides, you don't ▮ an audience! That will probably only ▮ stress without helping you and the o▮ person make up.

5. **Be very specific about the hurt ▮ caused.** Saying "I'm sorry I spread a ru about you" is better than "It's too bad s▮ people are so gossipy."

6. **Say it like you mean it.** If you just ▮ the words and aren't sincerely sorry, t▮ disrespectful. Plus, it makes it harde▮ people to trust you.

7. **Make a plan.** After your apology has ▮ offered and (hopefully) accepted, talk ▮ your friend about how to prevent the p▮ lem from happening again.

Need to Know?

Between a Rock and a Hard Place **by Alden R. Carter.** When Mark and Randy set off on a canoe trip, they learn about more than wilderness survival skills. As the guys face challenges together, they learn what it takes to be someone who can be counted on.

Boys Know It All: Wise Thoughts and Wacky Ideas from Guys Just Like You **by Michelle Roehm.** Thirty guys have written chapters with helpful hints on all kinds of important topics, including friendships. Check it out for advice on dealing with rough patches between friends.

A Smart Girl's Guide to Friendship Troubles: Dealing with Fights, Being Left Out, and the Whole Popularity Thing **by Patti Kelley Criswell.** From cyberbullying to mistreatment by so-called friends, this book has a lot of advice for girls figuring out social dilemmas. Tips, quizzes, and real-life stories about girls who've solved friendship problems can help you handle your own.

If you sense something's not right with a friend, do something about it. That doesn't mean you need to get in the person's face and have a big confrontation. No way! In fact, getting loud and angry hardly ever helps a situation.

Instead, talk with your friend and listen until you both understand where each of you is coming from. When you do that, you are probably going to feel respected and better about the situation. Does that guarantee that you'll never have to clear the air again? No, but from time to time every friendship hits rough spots. That's not necessarily a big deal because strong relationships don't break easily. **The faster you and a friend clear up any troubles, the faster you can get the friendship back to where it needs to be.**

"MY GOOD FRIEND MOVED. I STILL WANT TO BE HER FRIEND, BUT MY OTHER FRIENDS DON'T LIKE HER AND WANT ME TO DUMP HER. I SAID I'D THINK ABOUT IT. HELP!"
—NORI, 13

WELCOME TO "SHOULD I OR SHOULDN'T I?," WHE EXPERTS ADVISE TEENS UNDER PRESSURE.

SOUNDS LIKE NORI FEELS STUCK IN THE MIDDLE.

Should I OR Shouldn't I?

EXPERTS . . . WHAT DO YOU THINK NORI SHOULD DO?

SHE SHOULD TELL HER FRIENDS TO BACK OFF. THEY DON'T OWN HER.

TRUE, BUT THAT MIGHT MAKE THEM MAD.

FRIENDS SHOULDN'T PRESSURE YOU. THAT'S DISRESPECTFUL.

SO IS SAYING, "I'LL THINK ABOUT IT." WHY NOT TELL THE TRUTH?

'CAUSE THEY MIGHT DUMP HER.

SO WHAT SHOULD SHE DO?

WE'RE NOT SURE YET.

WELL, HURRY UP!

QUIT PRESSURING US

UH, TIME FOR A BREAK, BUT WE'LL BE BACK.

PRESSURE can make you

feel like you're being rushed or forced into making choices before you've had time to think things through. It can be uncomfortable, but it doesn't automatically mean that people are trying to get you to do something wrong.

For example, parents, teachers, or coaches might push you to take harder classes, enter a contest, or play a new position. That kind of pressure might give you a chance to stretch yourself in new directions. You may be unsure about something at first, but after thinking about it, you might realize, "Hey! That could be a good thing. I'll try it." The same goes for a friend who tries to get you to go out and do something fun if you're feeling down. That's a good kind of pressure.

But suppose, in order to say "yes" to someone, you have to go against what you believe in. That can make you feel like you're being pulled in two directions at once. If you've been in a situation like this, you might have thought that there weren't any good options. ("If I say yes to him I'm going to have to lie to my other friends. If I say no, he's going to tease me.") This kind of internal pressure can make it feel like you're at war with yourself.

From the "Quit pressuring me . . ." FILES

"Each time I talk to my best friend, we end up fighting because it's like she wants me to be more like her and do everything she likes to do. I've tried to explain myself over and over to her. I can't do it anymore."
—Ellie, 12

"I really don't want to drink, but sometimes I go to places where people are doing that. I kind of feel pressured to join in because I'm the only sober person there."
—Carl, 14

"My friend invited me to her party, but then we had a fight. She's trying to make me not want to come by saying things like, 'My mom doesn't like you.' I still want to go but I don't like what she's doing."
—Rachel, 11

"This one friend tried to get me to smoke. I said no, but he kept bugging me."
—Tomás, 13

"There's this guy I'm good friends with, but he likes me as more than a friend. I've told him many times that I don't want to go out with him. When I tell him, though, I don't think he takes me seriously."
—Wanda, 14

4 TIPS FOR DEALING WITH PRESSURE

1. **Identify the cause.** Get really cle on what's bothering you by putting into words. For example, try compl ing this sentence: Someone wa _____ but it doesn't feel rig because _____.

2. **Take a break.** Nap for a while. Pl with your cat. Hop in the show Whatever relaxes you is a good thi as long as it's safe and healthy. Rela ing can help calm your body and mi so you can think about solutions.

3. **Weigh your options.** If you're feeli torn between what someone expec of you and what you want, it c help to write down both sides of t tug-of-war. Being fully honest abc these pros and cons can help you s what's right.

4. **Take a stand.** Decide what you belie in and what you don't. Then tell of ers so there's no confusion. Wh your decisions reflect who you rea are, you can make peace with yo self and strengthen yourself agai negative pressure.

Where Do You Stand?

1. Has a friend ever convinced you to do something that you knew was wrong?
   Y or N

2. Have you ever felt you had to buy something just because a friend had it?
   Y or N

3. Have you kept yourself from doing what you thought was right because you knew your friends wouldn't like it?
   Y or N

4. Have you ever dropped an old friend because new friends didn't like the person?
   Y or N

5. Have you pretended that something was okay with you when you actually felt pressured?
   Y or N

6. Have you ever changed the way you dress or act to impress new people?
   Y or N

7. Have you made fun of someone because others were doing it?
   Y or N

8. Have you ever quit an activity because a friend quit or said you should?
   Y or N

If you got:

6–8 No answers: Peer pressure is rarely a problem for you. You know your values can stick to them. Others probably know this about you, too.

3–5 No answers: Sometimes you give in to negative peer pressure and you like you're not being true to yourself. But more and more you're letting your val guide you.

0–2 No answers: You don't stand up for your values as often as you could. Start be honest with yourself and your friends and peer pressure won't get to you as much.

s not your job to please
erybody. Your job is to live
ur life so you feel good about
o you are. If you want that for
urself, it can help to get really
ar on your values—the ideas
u and your family have about
at's right and what's not. And
 important to stick to those
ues. Why? Because knowing
at you believe in makes you
ong. Even if people try to push
u in directions that don't seem
ht, you remain steady. Also,
en you know what you value
st, there's no need to defend
You can just tell people, "Yes, I
I do that." Or, "No thanks. Not
 me."

Of course, even if you know
at's right for you, it's not
ays easy to say it. Especially
en someone you really care
out is pressuring you to do
nething different. But you can
nd your ground and speak up.
en you do, you'll be showing
urself respect, and probably
ning the respect of others.

WHO SAYS YOU SHOULD?

It can be hard to know what to do when a friend wants something different from what's best for you. These steps can help:

1. **Complete this statement:** "I think I should _____."

2. **Tell the truth about how you feel.** (The truth often reflects one of your strong values.) Here's an example: "I think I should stick with my old friends no matter what." But maybe the truth is: "I feel like my friends have changed and I don't like it when they try to get me to do certain things."

3. **Think about how you might be contributing to the pressure you feel.** Are you:
   —Staying silent instead of speaking up?
   —Pretending something is okay with you when it isn't?
   —Lying to yourself and others about what you really want?

4. **Ease the pressure.** You might:
   —Make a list of your values when it comes to family, friends, and school. That will remind you where you really stand.
   —Talk with the person pressuring you and express your true feelings.
   —Try to make choices that reflect what you truly believe.
   —Get support from someone who shares your values.

ealing with
RESSURE

"... friend called me names in front of ...yone for being afraid to smoke with ... I felt really pressured and out of ...e. Finally I told her I didn't want to ... to her level.'"

...heresa, 12

"... friend and I were being bullied by ...her kid. Finally I said 'Hey, why are ... picking on us?' And the guy said, ...ause I can. Do you have a problem ... it?' I told him the only reason he ...ed on us was so he could take out ... anger from his problems on other ...le. He hasn't bothered us since.'"

...lejandro, 11

"...riend was pestering me to tell her ...ething that this guy told me. If she ...w, I worried the information would ... around school. And my guy friend ...ld never forgive me for the taunting ... get. I didn't tell her.'"

...obbi, 14

"...ecided not to have anything to do ... this kid who drinks all the time. He ...d to get me to start, but I realized ... was a friend, he wouldn't be pres-...ng me to do something I don't want ...o.'"

...arlos, 13

"... you really don't want to, you don't ... to. No one can force you to do any-...g. If you're afraid you'll lose friends, ... are already lost to you. It can help ...sk, 'Why would you want me to do ... 'Why do you think it's cool?' 'Why ... you get it into your head that I ...'t want to?'"

...a, 13

MOUNTAIN POSE

This yoga pose can help you feel calm, strong, centered, and solid ... like a mountain. If you've never done yoga before, don't worry. This is a pose for beginners.

1. Take off your shoes and socks and stand on a bare floor.

2. Place your feet a few inches apart with the outer edges parallel.

3. Let your arms hang at your sides. Relax any tension in your elbows, wrists, and fingers.

4. Press your shoulders down and back. Open up your chest by lifting up your breastbone.

5. Press your tailbone (at the base of your spine) toward the ground.

6. Tilt your chin slightly downward to open the bones in the back of your neck.

7. Find a spot on the floor about five feet in front of you, and gently rest your eyes there.

8. Imagine a straight line from the base of your spine up through the top of your head.

9. Inhale and exhale slowly and evenly through your nose.

10. As you stand in this pose, imagine that you are a mountain. Imagine that your values keep you solid and anchored to the earth. Storms may blow all around, but the mountain stands tall and firm.

Need to Know?

Above the Influence (www.abovetheinfluence.com). It isn't always easy to disagree with your friends. It takes guts to stick to your values. This site offers support for dealing with peer pressure. You'll also find video stories from other teens on how they stay true to themselves.

The Courage to Be Yourself: True Stories by Teens About Cliques, Conflicts, and Overcoming Peer Pressure edited by Al Desetta with Educators for Social Responsibility. In 26 first-person stories real teens write about their lives with total honesty. Hearing their truths may inspire you to reflect on your life, work through challenges of your own.

Hot Issues, Cool Choices: Facing Bullies, Peer Pressure, Popularity, and Put-Downs by Sandra McLeod Humphrey. What do you do if pressure from a friend won't let up? What about people who put you down? This book offers solutions to real issues many teens face every day.

From time to time, even real friends will pressure each other in ways they shouldn't. When that happens, it doesn't necessarily mean that you can't trust someone or that you have to end a friendship. If you're feeling uncomfortable because a friend (or anyone) tries to get you to do something that isn't right for you, speak up. That's not always as easy as it sounds, but real friends will try to understand where you're coming from. Good things can happen when you're honest. For one, you'll feel good about being your own person. For another, you just might inspire a change in the thinking of other people (which could help them, too). **Even if you don't convince them of anything, standing up for yourself can gain you their respect.**

NEVER EATS. ALWAYS EXERCISING!?

HEY, MICHELLE. YOU ALL RIGHT?

HUH? YEAH. MATEO, EVER HAD A FRIEND WITH A PROBLEM YOU COULDN'T TALK ABOUT?

THEN I TRIED TELLING MY DAD 'CAUSE HE'S A COP AND HELPS KIDS. BUT I COULDN'T. AND JOE GOT IN WORSE TROUBLE.

YEAH, A SHOPLIFTING FRIEND. I TOLD HIM TO STOP, BUT HE DIDN'T.

WOW.

WHAT SHOULD I DO?

Everyone gets into situations at times where they feel lost, confused, or overwhelmed. That's when a friend's help can be huge. Even if you or the other person can't "fix" what's wrong, having someone to talk with can remind you both that you're not alone.

What if you suspect a friend has a problem, but she's never actually said anything? Or suppose she does mention it and then swears you to secrecy? What if the person sincerely believes there's no problem? If you think there is, then that becomes a problem for you.

Helping people who don't want your help—or who say they don't need it—is often very tricky. How can you be a real friend when helping might make someone upset with you?

GUESS I'M NOT THE ONLY ONE WITH THIS PROBLEM.

"What's a friend supposed to do?"

"My best friend started hanging out with this girl who smokes. Now he's smoking every day! Whenever I talk to him about it he gets mad and starts swearing. Other people say to let it go, but I can't."
—Jon, 13

"My friend's parents always make her stay home and watch her three-year-old sister. She never has time to herself. I guess her parents need help, but shouldn't she get to go out sometimes? I can tell it bugs her a lot, but she won't talk about it. I want to help her but I don't know how."
—Michael, 14

"One of our friends thinks this new is her best friend in the world. W shown proof that this girl spreads but our friend says we just hav gotten to know her yet. How can make sure our friend doesn't get hu
—Julie, 11

"I'm really worried about one of guy friends because he's started cut himself. When I ask him what's wro he says, 'Nothing's wrong, I'm fine!' afraid because he's hurting him What can I do?"
—Holly, 13

Sometimes what friends say they want and what they actually need may be very different. If you ever feel weighed down by something, that's a clear signal that you need to take action. A friend may not like that you've spoken up, but you may not be happy with yourself if you don't. More important, staying silent may keep someone from getting the help you know that person really needs.

From the "Helping a Friend" FILE

"My friend quit caring about the things he used to be interested in. Another friend and I asked him about what was going on. He wasn't necessarily happy at first, but after we talked I could tell he felt relieved. To this day, he appreciates our help."
—Don, 12

"When my friend's parents were going through a divorce it put a lot of stress on her. I spent time with her and just listened to her talk about her feelings. In some ways I feel that it helped her relieve stress."
—Selena, 11

"When my friend told me she wanted to kill herself, I went straight to an adult. After that she ignored me for a while, but today she thanks me for acting before anything could happen."
—Jake, 13

"I noticed cuts on my best friend's wrist and tried to talk her into telling her mom. She said she didn't want to tell anyone. I was scared that if I said anything she would cut herself even more. But if I kept it a secret, she'd probably keep cutting herself. I had no choice but to tell the counselor."
—Marianne, 14

ow Can OU Help?

en a friend's health is at , it's important to take on. Here are some of your st helpful options:

Educate yourself. Learn what you an about the situation your friend s dealing with. You might talk with thers who can tell you more about what's really going on.

Know your limitations. It's important that those who are in danger et the help of a doctor or counelor. You can and should support friend, but the person also needs o see a professional.

Talk to a trusted adult. If a friend sn't getting help, tell an adult right way. Even if someone swore you o secrecy, speak up. Talk to an adult at home or school. You can also call the National Youth Crisis Nineline (1-800-999-9999) or another helpline to get the person help. Whatever you do, don't allow problem to remain secret.

When it's time to get help for a friend . . .

National Sexual Assault Hotline (1-800-656-4673). Abuse is mistreatment. It can be physical, sexual, verbal, and emotional. If someone you know has been harmed or is in danger, tell an adult or call this 24-hour number.

National Suicide Prevention Lifeline (1-800-273-8255). More than a million American teens suffer from depression. Unfortunately, many don't realize they can find help. If you or a friend experiences suicidal feelings, people at this 24/7 number can help.

National Eating Disorders Association Helpline (1-800-931-2237). It can be hard to know what to do when someone is affected by an eating disorder. Remember: The health of you and your friends is what's most important. If you're not sure who you can talk to, call this helpline. Trained professionals are available Monday through Friday from 8:30–4:30 PST.

Need to Know?

The Cool Spot
www.thecoolspot.gov
Knowing the facts about alcohol and peer pressure can help you stay strong in making healthy choices. At the same time you can learn how to help friends do the same. The Cool Spot has information on these and other important topics.

TeensHealth
www.teenshealth.org
The Q&A section is filled with information you can use to support friends facing tough situations. Visit the site for advice on all kinds of health issues, including eating disorders, cutting, and substance abuse.

When you take action to help a friend, he might thank you right away. He may also get angry—and stay that way for a while. Even if someone doesn't appreciate your efforts, helping the person is still the right thing to do. That might be hard to remember, especially if a friend stops talking to you. But if you can do something to help someone you care about, it's important to do that.

Chapter 5: So-Called Friends

Real Friends vs. the Other Kind

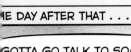

GOTTA GO TALK TO SOMEONE. HOLD THESE, OKAY?

UH . . .

NO PROBLEM.

WEEK LATER . . .

MONIQUE, CAN I TALK TO YOU ABOUT SOMETHING?

OH, SHOOT. IT'S 3:20! GOTTA RUN HOME BUT BE RIGHT BACK.

WHY IS SHE GOING THAT WAY WHEN SHE LIVES IN THE OTHER DIRECTION?

BONK!

Maybe you never thought about this, but you and your friends are equally responsible for what happens in your relationship. That includes the great times you share together and the not so great.

Feeling like you're in a lopsided friendship can be a problem. If you're the one getting second-rate treatment, it may help to own up to your part of what's going on. Tell friends the truth instead of saying nothing or letting them think that what they're doing is okay with you when it really isn't.

I'VE DONE SOME OF THIS PRETENDING.

PRETENDED WAS OKAY

"...ave friends who use the term ...' when they mean something is 'stupid.' ...tally and utterly disapprove, but I just go ...h' or pretend I agree with them."
...lberto, 13

"... friends and I often want to do differ- ...things. I usually give in and do what they ...t to avoid conflict. I don't want to get ...m angry at me."
...rin, 12

"...metimes people I care about drink or ...oke and ask if it's okay with me. I tell ...m that it's their life. But I really want ...ell them it's not okay. It makes me feel ...ly bad about myself, but I can't tell them ...real opinion."
...atrice, 14

"...y friend copies off my paper. I say yes so ...on't be bothered with the constant beg- ...g. I feel mad because I did all this work ...now someone is copying it."
...ictor, 11

"...was sitting with a guy friend and he was ...ing horrible slurs about different people. ...ew it wasn't okay, but I didn't say any- ...ng. I'm ashamed that I didn't try to ...p him."
...handra, 13

"...ve been upset with myself for pretending ...dn't care when my friends were really ...an to me. The truth is I cared a whole lot."
...atalie, 12

GETTING THE TREATMENT YOU DESERVE

A friend who regularly makes you feel uncomfortable probably isn't going to stop unless you say something about it. That might not be easy, but you owe it to yourself and the relationship. Here are some ideas to keep in mind:

1. **Remember: Your friends aren't mind readers.** People don't auto- matically know how you think or what you need. It's important to let friends know how you feel.

2. **Think about your part in the prob- lem.** Going along with what someone says when you don't agree, or staying silent when you aren't comfortable, can send the wrong message.

3. **Think about how you've tried to fix the problem.** Remember all the solutions you've tried to make things better with a friend. Have any of these attempts helped the situation? Made it worse?

4. **Brainstorm.** Come up with some new ideas for dealing with the prob- lem. You always have options. For example, if you're always the one to pay for activities, tell your friend that from now on you're only willing to pay for your share.

5. **Talk to someone.** Feeling brain dead? Bring up the issue with some- one you trust who's not involved in the situation. Getting another per- spective can help you come up with new solutions.

It can hurt to wonder whether someone really is your friend or not—especially if you thought the two of you were close. If you are questioning a friend's loyalty, pay attention to what you're feeling, because there's a reason for it. You may not know exactly why someone is acting a certain way. But if the person has done or said something that makes you think, "That's not right or fair," don't ignore it. **When something doesn't feel okay, it probably isn't.**

THEY'RE AS CONFUSED AS I AM!

From the "What's Going On?" FILES

"My friends have started leaving me out of stuff and acting like I misunderstood the plans. I'm sick of being the freak-ish pickle on a hamburger that everyone throws away!"
—Tamara, 13

"With my so-called best friend, it's like I'm paying for everything. Sometimes I feel like the only reason he wants me to be around is that there's no one else to do anything with."
—Sam, 12

"My friend promised she'd call and tell me why she was angry so we could talk about it. She has not kept that promise. She's lied to me at least four times."
—Kim, 12

"My best friend has changed since he found out that I like this girl. Now instead of making me feel better he says things like, 'You really need to get over yourself. She obviously hates you.' So I'm getting really mad. And it's making me distant from the guy I thought was my best friend in the world."
—Leo, 14

"My best friend has stopped acknowledging me around popular people. We talk on the phone, but only about homework."
—Sun, 11

What Would You Do?

1. **When your friend gets upset, she always takes it out on you. You:**
   a) say nothing because you don't want to make her angrier.
   b) tell her you've had enough and mean it.

2. **A friend keeps canceling plans with you at the last minute. You:**
   a) pretend it's no problem when he cancels.
   b) tell him that you can't count on what he says anymore.

3. **You don't really want to do something your friends are doing. You:**
   a) let them talk you into it.
   b) say, "I'll pass. You guys go ahead without me."

4. **Your friends always play video games and you're getting bored with it. You:**
   a) keep playing the same games with them.
   b) call other friends sometimes to switch things up.

5. **Your two best friends are fighting about something stupid. You:**
   a) pretend to agree with whatever they say so they don't get mad at you.
   b) declare yourself a "neutral zone" and refuse to join in the fighting.

6. You've been letting a friend copy your homework but it really bugs you. You:

  a) continue letting him cheat off of you.

  b) tell him you have to put an end to the copying.

7. Your friends ditched you (again), then blamed you for "getting lost." You:

  a) keep hanging out with these so-called friends (when you can find them).

  b) start looking for better friends ASAP.

8. Your friend always borrows money but never pays you back. You:

  a) keep forking over cash.

  b) tell him, "Sorry, but this ATM is closed."

9. Your ex-best friend is spreading rumors about you. You:

  a) pay the person back with worse rumors about her.

  b) talk directly to the person and get to the bottom of it.

10. You and your friend agree to run every Thursday. After a time your friend calls it quits and tries to get you to stop. You:

  a) quit running.

  b) keep your agreement with yourself.

If you got:

7–10 Bs: Most of the time you have no problem speaking up for yourself. You value honesty and it shows in the kind of friend you are. Nice going!

3–6 Bs: Sometimes you let friends talk you into things you're not comfortable with. But you're learning that you feel more confident in yourself when you make your own choices.

0–2 Bs: It's often a challenge for you to tell friends how you really feel. The next time you're in one of those situations, try taking a few deep breaths and standing firm. You might find that you're stronger than you thought!

WHAT HAPPENED YESTERDAY? YOU DIDN'T COME BACK OR ANSWER MY TEXTS.

YOU TEXTED ME?

ONLY ABOUT TEN TIMES.

HUH! I DIDN'T KNOW. OH, I FORGOT! MY BATTERY'S DEAD.

RING RING

I SWEAR IT WAS!

RING

HELLO?

UH, HOLD ON.

CAN YOU ASK JACK IF HE LIKES ME?

THAT WOULD FEEL WEIRD.

DOES THAT MEAN YOU WON'T?

IS THAT WHY WE'RE FRIENDS? SO YOU CAN GET TO JACK?

NO! IT'S 'CAUSE YOU'RE SO NICE.

IF "NICE" MEANS I LET YOU USE ME, THEN I'M NOT THAT NICE.

FINE. I'LL ASK HIM MYSELF.

JOURNAL

WHATEVER.

It can be a little scary to think about standing up for yourself—especially if a friend is on the bossy side and you've gotten used to falling in line. If you're feeling like you want to make a change, remember that you get to decide what kind of people you hang out with. If a relationship feels off balance, you don't need another person's permission to search for friends who will show you more respect. **You have the power to do that all by yourself.**

oing what's right for YOU

"f it feels wrong, then obviously some-ing is wrong. If I say that I don't think vhat's happening is funny or cool, the behavior usually comes to a screech-g halt. I think it's making the people I hang out with better people, too."
—Sylvia, 13

"When it comes to 'bad' friends, sometimes I think, 'Are these people worth lying to myself for?' Usually the answer is no and in the future I know to avoid it. My mother says if it's not the real you doing the action, it's not worth it because the results won't be true."
—Kahlil, 12

Sometimes I say things that n't true so my friends will like When they remind me of what id, I try to make up something to cover up. I feel like I'm just ng or saying whatever I can to press people. But then a voice ny head says, 'Why should you 'e what these people think? If y truly care about you then it shouldn't matter.'"
—Ron, 11

"I used to get mad at my friend a lot for things she did, but I wouldn't say anything. Now I've learned I don't like pretending, so I don't. Instead I get issues out in the open."
—Julee, 14

WHEN IT'S NOT WORKING

If you're tired of how a friend is acting toward you, it might be time for some changes. These tips can help:

1. Identify the problem. Think about exactly what someone is doing. Fill in the blank: I feel disrespected when my friend _____

2. Think about how the behavior makes you feel. You might feel hurt, angry, used, invisible, or any number of other ways. When your friend does what you said in #1, how do you feel?

3. Ask yourself why you put up with the behavior. Because they're your friends? Well, real friends don't disrespect each other, so maybe they're not actually on your side.

4. Take a direct approach. Talk privately and honestly with anyone who isn't showing you respect. You might say something like, "This has to stop, otherwise I can't be your friend anymore." Easy? Probably not, but absolutely necessary.

5. Keep a lookout. Old habits have ways of popping up again. When you see the same old behavior, in yourself or someone else, don't ignore it. That may have been part of the problem to begin with.

6. Stay true to your word. If the bad treatment continues, end the friendship. Showing respect for yourself is the first step toward getting it from others.

Need to Know?

Chillin': A Guy's Guide to Friendship by **Michael A. Sommers.** Even guys who usually get along great with each other can hit bumps in the road. This book has information for those tough times when competitiveness, popularity, or other issues make it hard for buddies to get along.

Lemonade Mouth by **Mark Peter Hughes.** Five of the school's most picked-on kids join forces to become a great band. Empowered by their newfound acceptance, these band members help other students make changes in the way they treat others.

The Girls' Guide to Friends: Straight Talk for Teens on Making Close Pals, Creating Lasting Ties, and Being an All-Around Great Friend by **Julie Taylor.** Do you have friends who cancel plans with you if someone or something "cooler" comes along? This book has advice for situations like this and many others. Quizzes and tips make it a helpful read.

Doing favors for people and being understanding when they mess up are part of what it means to be a real friend. But if you start to feel like you're doing all of the giving (and forgiving) and another person is doing all of the getting (and forgetting), something's probably out of balance. Maybe you're even unknowingly making the situation worse. If you try hard to understand what's going on, you can begin to recognize how your own behavior may be adding to the problem. That can help you figure out what you need to do.

Change isn't always easy, but it's an opportunity to make a situation better.

Maybe you've had a crush or two. Or maybe you've never really liked anyone in that way.

Perhaps you know someone who likes you, but you don't really feel the same. All of these situations are common. Having feelings for other people can come at different times—and those feelings can go away just as quickly.

Still, if your school is like many others, you and your friends may spend time talking and texting about who likes who. Maybe you're trying to figure out how a certain person feels about you right now.

DOES MY CRUSH LIKE ME?

I WONDER ABOUT THIS, TOO!

"She really doesn't flirt with every guy. But she is very friendly so it's hard to tell if she is flirting. I might ask her to the winter dance, but I'm worried because I don't know if she likes me."
—Patrick, 13

"I know he likes me as a friend, but I want to know if he likes me as something more. Some days he acts like he likes me a lot, and other days he acts like we just met."
—Marietta, 14

"My friends say that she likes me, but I'm not sure if they're lying. Sometimes she talks to me, but other times it seems like she's ignoring me. She smiles at me a lot, but I'm not exactly sure that counts as flirting."
—Christopher, 12

"My friend turned down this boy and then he asked me out. I was happy but the same day he dumped me. I still like him but I don't know if he asked me out just because my friend rejected him or if he really likes me."
—Pia, 14

"I have a huge crush on my guy friend. He and I are like glue to paper, the sun in the sky, the cable in a cable box. He might just think of me as one of his close friends. But, we do have so much fun ... He might feel the same way, but I just don't know."
—Hallie, 11

What Do the Signs Say?

How, or even if, people show their feelings varies a lot from person to person. Generally speaking though, you may get some clues if you read the "signs."

1. **Do you "get the feeling" that your crush likes you?** Does the person make eye contact? Smile at you? Laugh at your jokes? Try to make you laugh?

2. **Does this certain someone do nice things for you without being asked?** Little kindnesses can sometimes show that a person thinks you're special.

3. **Does the person go out of the way to be near you?** Does your crush come over to where you're standing? Change seats to be next to you?

4. **Does your crush show interest in getting to know you?** Does the person ask you personal questions? Really listen when you answer? Remember what you've said?

5. **Does the person treat you differently from everyone else?** If your crush flirts with everyone, it might be hard to tell if the person thinks you're "special."

If you got three or more "yes" answers, then there's a good chance your crush could be interested. Mostly "no" answers may mean the feelings you have aren't shared—or the person is doing a really good job of hiding them!

Some people are interested in dating. Some aren't.
And when it comes to the whole topic, parents can also have
different opinions. The adults in your family might be okay with you going out with someone. Or they might think you're not old enough. Maybe school dances or going out in groups are okay, but that's all. Whatever your situation, remember that you shouldn't let any pressure to join the dating scene influence you. If you're not ready to date, that's cool. Even if you are ready, knowing when and how to actually ask someone out can still be tricky.

Should I
TELL MY CRUSH how I feel?

"A year ago, my crush and I sort of flirted, but I wasn't ready to go out. Now, he doesn't act the same way around me. I don't know how to let him know that I like him without getting rejected too badly if his feelings have changed."
—Kim, 14

"I know a girl that likes me. I just don't know how to ask her out. I freeze up and don't know what to say."
—Juan, 12

"There's this guy that I really like. He said that he wanted us to be better friends before he asked me out. I'm cool with that, but he's always busy. I don't know how he really feels about me. Do I make the first move, or what?"
—Shannon, 13

"Quite a few girls like to hang out with me because I listen to what they have to say, but this can get in the way. Right now the girl I like is a good friend of mine. I want to ask her out but I'm afraid she'll say, 'I don't want to ruin our friendship.'"
—Enrique, 13

"I like this one boy, but I'm afraid if I ask him out he'll laugh at me."
—Germaine, 12

"I've had a crush on this girl for over a year, but it seems like I get on her nerves. It doesn't help that I'm overweight and don't know much about her. I really want to ask her out, but I'm afraid of rejection."
—Jason, 14

8 Questions for Deciding Whether to Ask Someone Out

If you're thinking of asking out your crush, here are some questions to consider before you make your move. They might not all fit for you, but some may be helpful in deciding:

1. Are you ready to date? If you feel like you may not be, you're probably right. If you feel like you are ready, be sure it's okay with parents or other adults at home.

2. Do you know each other well? If you aren't sure how your crush feels, then you may not know the person well enough. Before you ask anyone out, try to read the "signs" (see page 59).

3. Why not develop a friendship first? Take your time becoming friends. That way you'll know if you actually enjoy hanging out with the person.

4. How might it affect a friendship? If you and your crush are already close friends, that's great! But if your friend doesn't feel the same about you, the friendship may be affected.

5. What if your crush says no? Whenever you tell someone how you feel, you risk rejection. That's a fact of life. You may decide it's worth the risk anyway.

6. What might people say? Ask someone out and people may begin to gossip about you. They also might not, but it's worth thinking about how you'd feel if they do.

7. How clear is your head? People can start to act a little weird when they have a crush. Make sure you're calm and avoid doing or saying anything you may later regret.

8. What if it doesn't last? It can be exciting to really like someone. But just as quickly as feelings come, they can also go. That's a natural part of crushes.

TO BE CONTINUED . . .

It would be great if the people we like instantly had the same feelings for us. Sometimes this does happen, but more often the other person has very different feelings—or maybe none at all. It's true that crushes are often temporary, but let's be honest: When you're in the middle of one and someone doesn't share your feelings, it's probably going to hurt a little. Maybe even a lot.

"My crush rejected me"

"I'm pretty sure the guy I'm interested in likes my friend. He asked for her number and email address today, and then I saw them walking together. I know it's not my friend's fault but it hurts anyway."
—Noelle, 14

"A few months ago I told this girl how I felt, and things have been weird ever since. She doesn't feel a fraction of what I feel for her. Is there some way I can lose these feelings or make her share them?"
—Tony, 14

"It makes me sick to see my crush with another girl. I want to stand by him as a friend, but it's painful to know it's not me that he really likes."
—Pat, 12

"I thought this boy I like liked me, too. But then I overheard him tell my friend that he would never go out with me."
—Brillianna, 13

"I got my friend to ask the girl I like whether she liked me. The answer was a definite no—she even said she hated me Now I'm miserable."
—Joey, 13

"My friends dared me to ask out this boy I like, but I was too afraid. Then my friend said that she would ask him out for me—even though I didn't want her to. She asked him anyway and he said no. I felt so humiliated."
—Cherylynn, 13

Getting Over a Crush

It can hurt a lot when someone doesn't share your feelings. Keeping these ideas in mind can help:

1. It's one person. There are other people you enjoy being around who appreciate you. If you need proof, make a list of those (including friends, parents, and relatives) who truly care about you.

2. Everyone's not perfect for one another. You may like the way a pair of shoes looks, but if they don't fit, it's just not a good match. It's the same with crushes. If someone rejects you, the two of you probably aren't a good match. The "right" person will want to spend time together as much as you do.

3. Breathe. Whenever you find yourself thinking about the person and feeling down, stop and take some deep breaths. Breathe in through your nose and think, "Breathing in." Breathe out through your mouth and think, "Breathing out." Repeat as many times as you need to feel better.

4. Get support. Friends can help you move past the rejection. Maybe they've had similar experiences or have advice to share. Hanging out with friends can also take your mind off a person and let you get back to enjoying other activities you really care about.

5. Take your time. The next time you have feelings for someone, get to know each other as friends before going out. When you take things slower, you can build more trust and respect between one another.

What Would a
Friend Do?

1. Your crush starts going out with your friend. You:

a) move on.

b) pretend that you're over it (when you're really not).

c) tell your crush how you feel.

d) pretend to like someone else to make the person jealous.

e) try to break up the new couple.

2. You like your best friend's ex. You:

a) ask if it's okay to go out with the person.

b) get advice from someone you trust.

c) try to get your friend to go out with someone new.

d) ask out your friend's ex in secret.

e) do nothing about the crush because you don't want to hurt your friend.

3. You and a friend like the same person. You:

a) flirt with the person to win more attention.

b) just act normal and see who the person likes best.

c) decide that the friendship is more important than any crush.

d) pretend you don't like the person so that your friend can make a move.

e) tell the person something negative about your friend.

4. You feel pressure from friends to ask out the person you like, but your mom won't let you date. You:

a) talk to your mom about the pressure.

b) give yourself some time to think about the situation.

c) do your best to become better friends with the person.

d) ask friends to stop pressuring you.

e) start dating the person without telling your parents.

5. Your best friend is going out with someone and seems to no longer have time for you. You:

a) pretend everything is cool when it isn't.

b) hang out with other single friends.

c) spread rumors about the person your friend is dating to break them up.

d) talk with your friend and set up a time when the two of you can hang out.

e) get angry with your friend but don't say why.

Answers:

1. **a.** Moving on isn't always easy, but it's a good way to preserve your friendship and your self-respect.

2. **a.** Asking how your friend feels makes sense. But even if the person says (and believes) it's okay, it may upset your friend to see you with an ex. **b.** Asking for advice is always a smart move. **e.** Sometimes choosing to do nothing is also smart.

3. **b.** or **c.** are the best options here. It all depends on what you and your friend decide between you. Just make sure you talk about it honestly.

4. **a. b. c. d.** These are all smart ways to respect yourself and your values. Talking through an issue will make a situation better for everyone. As for **e.** going against rules you have at home usually only complicates matters.

5. **b.** and **d.** make a winning combination. By doing both, you get to spend some time with other friends without losing your best friend or your self-respect.

Need to Know?

100 Things Guys Need to Know **by Bill Zimmerman.** It can be tough to know what to say or how to act around crushes. This book has conversation starters and other information on the subject, including tips like, "Be a friend first." There are also suggestions for being a respectful guy.

A Smart Girl's Guide to Boys: Surviving Crushes, Staying True to Yourself and Other Stuff **by Nancy Holyoke and Bonnie Timmons.** This book provides lot of advice for figuring out your feelings, dealing with competition, getting over jealousy, and more. You'll also find real letters from girls and good advice from guys.

If friends or other people in your school are dating, you may feel pressure to date, too. But you don't have to do anything. If you do start, it's best not to expect things to always go perfectly. They probably won't. Why? Most relationships have ups and downs. And getting to know other people can be awkward, especially when what you learn isn't what you expected. Or, you might be in the process of figuring out what you want for yourself. Introducing another person into the mix can make that more difficult. **The bottom line: When it comes to dating, doing what's right for you and standing by your values gives you the best chance at having the life you want.**

Real friends are happy when a buddy finds something (or someone) that makes him happy. **But when a new activity (or person) suddenly takes up a lot of someone's time, new challenges can come up between friends.** Strong feelings on all sides may make everyone involved distrustful of one another. **Working through these times might take some patience and understanding. It may also test the strength of the friendship.**

If you're feeling left out (or left behind), talk to the person about it. And be honest! **Pretending that you're fine with a situation isn't going to help anything. If you're the one feeling torn between spending time with someone other than your friend, talking about it can help you, too. What won't help is being dishonest with one another.**

THINGS CAN GET TOUGH BETWEEN FRIENDS.

"What's happening here?"

"My friend's girlfriend is always mad at him about something. Ever since he started going out with her he has been fading away from his other friends. The thing is, I don't think he's even happy with her. We all wish we could help him."
—Miguel, 14

"When my friend got a boyfriend there was suddenly no room for any of her friends. She would 'try' to make plans to catch up with us, but when the time arrived, no call, no nothing. I've told her she isn't being fair to her friends, but she always says I'm being mean. I'm sick of trying when there is no result."
—Bianca, 14

"My best friend and I have started following different interests and making new friends. That's cool with me. But lately, he ignores me like I'm some total stranger. I've brought it up before and he just shrugged it off. I don't even know if we're friends anymore."
—Kevin, 11

"My friend and I were super close, but this new girl came along and they became closer. She says it's because they have a lot in common. They even lie to me sometimes so they can hang out with each other. I miss my best friend!"
—Emily, 12

"My friend and I used to spend all of our time together, but ever since he got a girlfriend I don't ever see him. It seems like the ground rules we set as friends don't apply anymore."
—Edgar, 13

FAKE PROMISES

Real friends make real promises they intend to keep. Fake promises, on the other hand, can hurt others and damage a person's self-respect. Here are some tips to avoid fake promises in your friendships:

1. **Check in with your feelings.** If you're feeling a little guilty, pressured, or stressed, that may mean that you're about to make a promise that you don't think you'll keep. Try to stop yourself before a fake promise slips out.

2. **Check in with your thoughts.** If you're already thinking, "How can I get out of this?" or "I'll worry about this later," that could be a sign that you are agreeing to something you're not going to follow through on.

3. **Take a deep breath.** It can calm you down and get you back in touch with your values—including your intention to be a good friend.

4. **Tell the truth.** You may sometimes think you're being nicer by saying yes, but it's a lot more respectful to avoid making a promise you'll end up breaking.

5. **Say you need time to think about it only if you really do.** There's no point in saying that you "need time" when you know that even if you had a hundred years to think about it the answer would still be "no."

REAL or FAKE
PROMISE?

1. A friend begs to come to your birthday party, but you're at the limit of people you can invite. To make her be quiet about it, you say, "Okay. Whatever. I promi you'll be invited."

   Real or Fake?

2. Your friend has been bugging you to go with him to visit his cousin. You've always made excuses because you don't like the kid. But now your friend's ma and says you have to go. You roll your eyes and promise you will.

   Real or Fake?

3. Your best friend lends you her mp3 player so that you can talk to your parents about getting one. You promise to bring it back tomorrow.

   Real or Fake?

4. Recently your friend's been acting like he doesn't want to hang out with you anymore. You call him and right away he says, "I'll call you back in five minute

   Real or Fake?

5. You promise your best friend that tomorrow you'll bring in this really cool ma that your grandparents brought back from Japan. But then you forget.

   Real or Fake?

Answers:

It's hard to know for sure when a promise is real or fake. While there's no perfect wa tell the difference, some hints can make it easier.

1. This could be a fake promise because it doesn't seem like you'll be able to invite Time will tell, but it's best to be honest.

2. Hard to tell. Eye-rolling is often a sign of a fake promise. But, this time, because y friend's angry, you might actually mean what you say.

3. When someone does you a special favor, it's respectful to keep your promise. Si you're grateful to your friend, it's likely you'll return her player right away.

4. Since he hasn't been a great friend lately, it's probably reasonable to assume tha won't call you back like he promised.

5. You probably meant for this to be a real promise. Sometimes we slip up and nee apologize for not following through. How about putting the mask in your backp so you don't forget tomorrow?

If you feel like things aren't working out between you and someone else, it's likely that whatever is making you uncomfortable has been bothering you for a while. For example, suppose a friend keeps making plans with you and then leaving you behind. Or say someone has promised not to flirt with the guy (or girl) you like but keeps doing it anyway.

Depending on the situation, you may have good reasons to be annoyed with the other person. But there's another part to this equation . . . your part. If you're completely honest about how you got where you are, you may be angry with yourself for letting something slide again and again. **If a relationship is out of balance, it's important to take action that will make you feel better.**

"Things are changing . . ."

"A friend of mine and I were sitting next to each other at youth group and she had to go do something. The next thing I know another girl sits next to me. I never got the chance to talk to my friend for the rest of the meeting because this other girl was like glued to my side. I think my friend thinks that I like this girl much more than I do, and now she's acting all jealous. It's weird!"
—Andrew, 12

"When I earned my yellow belt in judo, my boyfriend just laughed. I was kinda mad and so I challenged him to a match. He didn't think he had to try hard against a girl, but I kept using throws and leg sweeps to send him to the floor. Now he's totally bent out of shape. I'm tired of his attitude and insulting comments."
—Jeanette, 14

"Slowly our relationship is deteriorating. We don't have much to talk about, and she hangs around other friends all the time. I don't fit in with them . . . therefore less time for me."
—Ken, 13

"My feelings for her are strong, but I want to spend more time with other people. I've tried breaking up with her, but she gets upset and I feel bad. I want to break up for good, but I don't know how to do it."
—Tyler, 13

"My friends mean the world to me but they don't like the guy I'm seeing. Yes, sometimes he and I fight over stupid things, but that's not the only part of the relationship. They want me to break up with him, and I feel like I'm stuck in the middle. I'm really unhappy and everyone's mad at me."
—Vivian, 14

How Do YOU FEEL?

A motion detector in front of an automatic door senses when you're walking toward it and switches to "Active" mode. In the same way, you can sense a change in your feelings and use it to become a better friend to yourself and others. Here's how:

1. **Notice shifts in mood.** Your feelings may suddenly change from neutral (calm) to some other feeling (like anger or sadness).

2. **Stop whatever you're doing.** Take a moment to focus on what you're feeling.

3. **Figure out exactly how you feel.** Be as accurate as you can. For example, are you just "mad" or are you actually feeling "mostly annoyed and a little bit frustrated with a side order of confusion"?

4. **Think about what triggered your mood change.** Was it something someone said or did? Are you unsure about a new relationship?

5. **Consider options.** How might you resolve the situation? Think about options you have for making yourself feel better.

YOUR RIGHTS

When it comes to going out with other people, remember:

1. **You have the right to feel safe.** It's important to feel physically and emotionally safe at all times when you're with another person. If you don't, get out of the situation ASAP.

2. **You have the right to be treated with respect.** You deserve the chance to express your thoughts and feelings. The other person should listen to and respect what you have to say.

3. **You have the right to your own time.** You can spend all the time you like away from another person—whether that's to hang out with friends, spend time with family, or do something on your own.

4. **You have the right to your body.** You shouldn't feel pressure when it comes to getting physical. It's your right to say no to hugging, kissing, and anything else.

5. **You have the right to end a relationship.** It doesn't matter what your reasons are. You don't have to justify how you feel to anyone.

If you feel confused about what to do, it can help to talk with an adult you trust. You can also call the Nineline (1-800-999-9999), a 24/7 helpline for teens.

Call it splitting up, breaking up, or getting dumped, the end of a relationship is usually not a lot of fun for anyone. It can feel pretty terrible when someone doesn't want to spend as much time together as you do, especially if you still have feelings for the person. And having to tell someone that you want to move on can be almost as difficult. Why? **BECAUSE HUMAN BEINGS CARE ABOUT OTHER PEOPLE.** There's actually a part of our brain that makes us feel sad when other people are unhappy. That's the same part that can make us uncomfortable when we hear bad news—or when we have to deliver bad news to others.

om the "Broken Up" FILES

trying to get over her, but I really miss
No one has hurt me this much ever!"
ony, 14

e went to the movies the night before he
ke up with me. It was really fun, so there
no reason for him to do what he did. Dur-
our relationship, I lost friends because I
't sit with them at lunch. Now I have no
to turn to."
andra, 13

e broke up because she made a mistake,
the next day she called a million times
I took her back. Two weeks ago I made a
ake and she broke up with me. It seems
we fight whenever she's with her friends."
oberto, 14

"My boyfriend just broke up with me online. I find it really irritating that he didn't do it in person. He tells me that we hardly talk. I try to have conversations, but lately he has been blowing me off to hang out with his friends."
—**Francine, 12**

"I wanted to know why my boyfriend was breaking up with me and he said that he heard something about me. So I asked, 'What did you hear?' He wouldn't tell me!"
—**Andrea, 13**

"This guy I was seeing said he was breaking up with me because he was doing really bad in school. He said he also had three hockey teams to deal with and that his parents were pressuring him. I'm not sure if this means we're taking a break or breaking up for good."
—**Diane, 12**

5 TIPS FOR BREAKING UP WITHOUT HURTING SOMEONE (TOO BADLY)

While there's no guaranteed way to end a relationship so that everyone's feeling fine, some breakup strategies are definitely more respectful and less hurtful than others. The most important thing to remember: Talk directly with the person you're going out with. It's no one else's business, unless you need help sorting out your feelings.

1. **Make sure you know why you want to break up.** Do you feel pressured to do things you're not comfortable with? Have your feelings for the person changed? Do you want to spend more time with friends? Whatever the reason, be clear on what it is before talking to the person.

2. **Think about what you're going to say.** Before you say anything, think about how it would feel to hear those words in that tone of voice.

3. **Don't say or do anything with the intention to hurt anyone.** No matter what your ex did (or what you think the person did) you don't have the right to be mean.

4. **Talk about how you feel.** Even if you feel like your ex wasn't especially nice to you, the real reason you're ending it is because of how you feel, not because of what the other person did.

5. **Stay strong.** Staying in a relationship longer than you want because you don't want to hurt someone's feelings is faking it. That's not respectful—to yourself or anyone else.

Moving On

• • • • • • • • • • • •

"I dated this girl for a year. We br[oke] up in August under good terms, [and] we've been excellent friends sinc[e.]"
—Danny, 14

"My best guy friend and I deci[ded] to go out together. Big mistake! [We] talked about it honestly, and bot[h of] us decided that we were much be[tter] as friends. A lot of people said w[e'd] ruin the friendship if we went [out.] But it turned out that our friend[ship] is stronger than ever."
—Raina, 14

"I moved and before I left I br[oke] up with my girlfriend. Because of [the] long-distance thing she underst[ood] and agreed it was a good idea."
—Byron, 13

"I broke up with my boyfriend [last] year because it wasn't working [out] (though he wanted to give it ano[ther] try). At first it was awkward betw[een] us because he still had feelings [for] me. But we actually got to be g[ood] friends."
—Josephine, 14

"We broke up in May and ever s[ince] we have still stayed friends. We [get] along most of the time, which ma[kes] me feel better about our decisio[n to] break up."
—Pascal, 13

Going out can create whole new challenges.

Maybe it's figuring out what you want or whether you're even ready. Perhaps it's dealing with pressure to choose between spending time with your friends and someone new. That might lead to trying to please everyone and feeling like you're not doing a very good job.

The reality is that relationships are often challenging—in the beginning, in the middle, and in the end. Another reality is that relationships can end. And when they do, there can be rough days and hurt feelings to deal with. But with time and space and effort, sometimes exes can become friends.

Even if it's hard, breaking up makes a lot more sense than putting up with a relationship that's not working. **It's important to always be honest with yourself and stick to your own values—no matter what another person might say.**

Chapter 8: Making New Friends

We all sometimes make snap decisions based only on a small bit of information that might not be true or show the whole picture. Our judgments about other people often happen so quickly, we may not even realize we're making them. For example, if a guy you don't know is reading a magazine with a unique cover, you might instantly form an opinion about him. If a new girl shows up in P.E. and plays basketball really well, you may immediately stick her with a label. We often make assumptions about people before we've even spoken with them.

Are these snap decisions fair? No, but that doesn't keep them from happening. We quickly size up people in a way that influences how we think about them. "He's a loser. I don't want anything to do with him." Or, "She's cool. I want to spend more time with her."

While we're making instant calls about people we don't know, they're doing the same thing about us.

From the "Labeled and Judged" FILES

"There's this guy at school who speaks in a different way. I assumed he was weird or something. But then one day we were talking and I found out he is hearing impaired. He's actually a really good guy and we've become friends."
—Charlie, 11

"This one guy in our grade is so short. At first I thought he must be a young kid who moved up two or three grades. Now that I've got to know him, I realize he's our age and likes a lot of the things I do. I feel bad that I jumped to conclusions about him."
—Marisa, 14

"This new girl came to school dressed all preppy and I thought she'd be really stuck up. But when we started talking, she wasn't like that at all. I felt stupid for judging her before she had even said two words."
—Vicente, 12

"There's this guy everyone calls a 'bad boy.' One day we started talking and he was actually really nice and sensitive—just a little rough around the edges. We've ended up becoming close friends. I wish other kids would see his softer side."
—Lilly, 13

Do **YOU** Make
Snap Decisions?

1. A new kid at school wears a style of shirt you've never seen before. You decide guy is strange.
   T or F

2. Your friends tell you that this one girl's mom drives a super fancy car. You dec that they must be rich.
   T or F

3. You find out a guy in your class likes jazz and decide he must be pretty cool.
   T or F

4. You hear this girl tell someone that she has a pet tarantula. You decide that s a liar.
   T or F

5. People are saying that this tall guy has been held back in school three times. decide he's either stupid or a troublemaker.
   T or F

6. You see a really pretty girl and decide she's probably too popular to want to h out with you.
   T or F

7. You're becoming friends with this new girl when you hear that she plays the t You decide that's dorky and stop being her friend.
   T or F

If you got:

5–7 Trues: Snap decisions have become a habit. They may be preventing you from ting to know people for who they are.

2–4 Trues: Quick judgments sometimes block you from seeing people as they really But you're learning that they aren't always true.

0–1 Trues: You're a fair and open-minded person who tries not to make snap decisi You are also probably friends with many kinds of people.

If you've ever felt like you didn't have enough friends, or enough of the real kind, you're not alone. Everyone has wished for more (or better) friends at some time or other—even really popular people who always seem to be surrounded by others.

Maybe you have a lot of people you're friendly with but not any close friends that you can fully trust. Or maybe you have a group of people you were close to who turned out to be not all that nice. Let's face facts: **Friendships aren't always easy. They can take work. If you'd like things to improve, thinking about changes you want is a good place to start.**

"I need new friends!"

SOME FRIENDSHIPS JUST DON'T WORK OUT.

"Whenever I'm mad at my friends for something, they never say sorry. That really ticks me off. I don't want to be friends with these people anymore, but who else will I hang out with?"
—**Carly, 11**

"My best friend stopped calling me. I understand that she might want to spend time with other people, but she totally ditched me. I've asked her why and she says it's called growing up. I feel like I've lost my sister."
—**Karyn, 12**

"My father is in the military and we have to move constantly. I've been able to make friends in other places we've been, but no such luck this time. We've been here for a year and I haven't made any friends!"
—**Preston, 13**

"My former friend ignores me in school. I wrote her about it in an email, but she just wrote back that I'm a loser. I said some nasty things about her after that, but then she posted really nasty rumors about me on her Web site. She got her friends to do it, too."
—**Carmen, 13**

"I used to have a lot of friends. But this year I've lost quite a few since I decided to avoid people who smoke or do drugs."
—**Blake, 13**

"I was so cool and popular in fifth grade. Then when middle school everything changed. I lost a 'friend' in s grade and another in seventh. I don't k why people just turned against me. I wo never do what they did to me."
—**Anthony, 14**

"Our whole eighth grade is fighting, espec the girls. They pretend to be your friends, if you say something they go and tell every What friends, huh? I wish we all could start over again."
—**Alison, 14**

"My best friend and I hardly talk anym He still says that we're friends but he just that because he knows it would hurt me i didn't. I want our old friendship back, but probably won't happen. I guess I need to m some new friends."
—**Mark, 12**

5 WAYS TO MAKE FRIENDS

Finding and keeping good friends is hard enough, but changing grades or schools can make it even more difficult. Maybe the people you used to hang out with aren't around anymore, or if they are, maybe you're not as close as you once were. There are plenty of reasons why you might be looking for new friends.

Of course, wanting friends and making them are two different things. For many people, starting new friendships can seem difficult. Half of the trick is having a positive attitude and being friendly. But the most important part comes from inside. When you know what kind of friend you want, and you know how to be that kind of friend, you're in good shape.

If you need some new friends, sitting around waiting for them to show up isn't much of a plan. Here are some ideas for finding new people to hang out with:

1. **Know what you're looking for.** Make a list of the qualities you need in a friend. Stick with what you want, not what you don't want. (For example: "I want a friend who is supportive," instead of "I don't want a friend who tells lies about me.") Make a long list and keep it positive.

2. **Do more of what you enjoy.** After-school sports and clubs are good places to make new friends. You'll automatically have at least one shared interest with everyone else there.

3. **Keep a lookout for positive people.** People who are friendly and quick to lend a helping hand are often open to making new friends. Of course, it works in both directions. If you want to show you're that kind of person, too, try to be kind and thoughtful.

4. **Change your attitude.** If your way of thinking tends to be negative, try turning the dial in a more positive direction. It's not always easy to do this, but others are more likely to make friends with those who are cheerful and upbeat. Is it hard for you to shake negative moods? Talk with someone you trust about how you feel.

5. **Perform service in the community.** You don't have to go far to find organizations that help people, animals, or the environment. See what appeals to you. By lending a helping hand after school or on weekends, you do good for your community. You'll also meet people who can become new friends.

"WHEN IT COMES TO FRIENDS . . ."

HERE ARE MORE FRIENDSHIP TIPS.

"Pick your friends right because good ones will stick with you until the end. If people change in ways you don't agree with, find others who share your values."
—Jorge, 12

"If you're mad at someone, they're probably mad at you, too. So work it out."
—Kerry, 11

"Don't ditch your friends. Also, don't be exclusive and hang out with one small group all the time. You may miss out on getting to know some great people."
—Stefanie, 14

"Don't be blind when people are doing something wrong. Part of the deal is that you and your friends tell each other the whole truth."
—Muhammad, 12

"Forgive friends if they mess up a few times. Be honest with them about how you feel."
—Danielle, 13

"Help your friends and they'll help you in the future. If you hurt others, it can come back to haunt you when you least expect it."
—Emmalynn, 13

"It doesn't matter if a certain crow doesn't think much of your friend They don't know them like you do. A long as you can count on people, that all that really matters."
—Chris, 12

"Having good friends is more importa than what clothes brand you are wea ing. Good friends don't go out of style
—May, 14

"If you have a good friend, you're luck If you don't, keep looking until yo find one."
—Said, 11

Hoot by Carl Hiaasen. Roy is the new kid at Trace Middle School. That means lunches alone in the cafeteria and no real friends to speak of. But all of that changes when a series of mysterious events leads him to discover a colony of burrowing owls—and his first true friend.

Tolerance
www.tolerance.org/teens
Often people around us have a lot more in common with us than we realize. This site has ideas for teens looking to bring seemingly different people together at school and in the community.

YMCA and YWCA
www.ymca.net
www.ywca.org
There's a Y in pretty much every part of the country. You can visit these Web sites for friend-finding activities that include sports, art classes, and teen leadership programs.

With two-way trust and respect, you and your friends can count on each other and have more fun all around. Sure, there will be ups and downs. That's part of every friendship. But as long as you know how to be the kind of friend you'd like to have, then you'll be fine. In fact, you'll be better than fine.

You'll be a great friend to yourself and everyone else.

Index

A

Above the Influence (Web site), 36
Acceptance, 10, 12
Advice, getting, 41, 47, 75
Advice, giving, 39, 42
Apologies, 26

B

Between a Rock and a Hard Place (Carter), 27
Boys Know It All (Roehm), 27
Brainstorming, 47
Breakups, 75–79
Breathing exercises, 20, 65, 71

C

Chillin' (Sommers), 55
Choices, making, 28–43
The Complete Idiot's Guide to Friendship for Teens (Lutz), 16
Conflicts, 17–27, 70–73
The Cool Spot (Web site), 43
The Courage to Be Yourself (Desetta), 36
Crushes, 56–68

D

Dating, 56, 60–63, 66–68, 75–79
Decision making, 30, 54, 81–82

E

Eating disorders, 41, 42
Exclusion, 49–51

F

Feelings, hurt, 64–65, 17–27
Feelings, sensing own, 15, 33, 49, 75
Forgiveness, 10, 25–27
Friends, making new, 80–89
Friendships, ending, 54–55, 69–79

G

The Girls' Guide to Friends (Taylor), 55
Gossip, 17, 19, 20

H

Health issues, 40, 41
Helping friends, 10, 37–43
Holes (Sachar), 16
Honesty, 10, 25, 33, 36, 70, 71
Hoot (Hiaasen), 89
Hot Issues, Cool Choices (Humphrey), 36
Hotlines, 41, 75
The How Rude! Handbook of Friendship & Dating Manners for Teens (Packer), 79

I

Insensitivity, 17–20, 21–25
The InSite (Web site), 1, 79

L

Lemonade Mouth (Hughes), 55
Listening, 40
Lying, 19, 49, 52

N

National Eating Disorders Association Hotline, 41
National Sexual Assault Hotline, 41
National Suicide Prevention Lifeline, 41
Nineline/National Youth Crisis Nineline, 41, 75

O

100 Things Guys Need to Know (Zimmerman), 68
Online advice, 1, 36, 43, 79, 89

P

Peer pressure, 28–36, 68
Pleasing others, 33
Promises, 69, 71–73

R

Real friends, 8–16, 23–25
Relationships, ending, 75–7⬤
Respect, 10, 18, 25, 34
Responsibility, taking, 26, 4⬤ 47
Revenge, 20
Rights, 75
Rumors, 19, 20

S

Secrets, telling, 19, 20
Self-respect, 33, 53
Sexual assault, 41
The Sisterhood of the Trave⬤ Pants (Brashares), 16
A Smart Girl's Guide to Be⬤ (Holyoke and Timmons),⬤
A Smart Girl's Guide to Friendship Troubles (Criswell), 27
Snap decisions, 81–82
So-called friends, 44–55
Standing up for self, 30–33⬤
Suicide, preventing, 40, 41
Support, 16

T

Teasing, 19, 20
TeensHealth (Web site), 43⬤
Tolerance (Web site), 89
Trust, 11, 12, 14, 15, 18

Y

YMCA and YWCA (Web sites), 89
Yoga, 35

out the Author

Annie Fox, M.Ed., graduated from Cornell University with a degree in Human Development and Family Studies and completed her master's in Education at the State University of New York at Cortland. After a few years teaching in the classroom, computers changed her life and she began to explore the ways in which technology could be used to empower teens.

Annie has since contributed to many online projects, including as creator, designer, and writer for the The InSite—a Web site for teens taking on life's challenges. Annie also answers questions for the Hey Terra! feature, an online advisor. Her Internet work has contributed to the publication of multiple books, uding *Too Stressed to Think?* and the Middle School Confidential series. Annie is available for ic speaking engagements and workshop presentations on teen and parenting issues.

When not answering Hey Terra! letters, Annie enjoys yoga, meditation, cooking, hiking, traveling, , most of all, spending time with her husband David and the rest of the family.

out the Illustrator

Matt Kindt was born in 1973 to a pair of artistically supportive parents. Living briefly in New York, Matt has spent most of his years in the Midwest, and the last 15 years in Webster Groves, Missouri, a suburb of St. Louis. In middle school, he would often create mini-comics featuring the teachers, to the delight of his fellow classmates. Matt is the Harvey Award–winning writer and artist of the graphic novels *Super Spy* and *2 Sisters* and co-creator of the Pistolwhip series. He has been nominated for four Eisner and three Harvey Awards. In addition to graphic novels, Matt also works as a freelance illustrator and graphic designer. When he is not working, Matt enjoys long trips to the playground with his wife and daughter.

Fast, Friendly, and Easy to Use
www.freespirit.com

Browse the catalog

Info & extras

Many ways to search

Quick check-out

Stop in and see!

1.800.735.7323 • fax 612.337.5050 • help4kids@freespirit.com

FOLLOW THE JOURNEY OF JACK, JEN, CHRIS, ABBY
MATEO, AND MICHELLE—SIX STUDENTS JUST TRYING
TO FIGURE IT ALL OUT IN MIDDLE SCHOOL . . .

BOOK 1
Be Confident in Who You Are

BOOK 2
**Real Friends vs.
the Other Kind**

BOOK 3
What's Up with My Fam

BOOK
COMING
SOON!

The Middle School Confidential™ series blends fiction and practical advice
a contemporary, graphic-novel format that will draw in even reluctant read
Includes quizzes, quotes from real kids, tips, tools, and resources. For ages 11-